quips and quotes

Americans

Instead of the Pilgrim Fathers landing on the Plymouth Rock, the Plymouth Rock should have landed on the Pilgrim Fathers.

Anonymous

No one ever went broke underestimating the intelligence of the American people.

H.L. Mencken

America is a nation that conceives many odd inventions for getting somewhere but can think of nothing to do when it gets there.

Will Rogers

The United States never lost a war or won a conference.

Will Rogers

October 12, the Discovery.

It was wonderful to find America, but it would have been more wonderful to miss it.

Mark Twain, *Following the Equator*

Of course America had often been discovered before Columbus, but it had always been hushed up.

Oscar Wilde,
Personal Impressions of America

It is absurd to say that there are neither ruins nor curiosities in America when they have their mothers and their manners.

Oscar Wilde

Appearance

Her heart's in the right place – what a pity the other thirteen stone aren't!

Anonymous

You're looking nicer than usual, but that's so easy for you.

Saki

It is only shallow people who do not judge by appearances.

Oscar Wilde, *The Picture of Dorian Gray*

It is better to be beautiful than to be good. But ... it is better to be good than to be ugly.

Oscar Wilde, *The Picture of Dorian Gray*

I was so ugly when I was born, the doctor slapped my mother.

Henny Youngman

Arguments

There are three sides to every argument:
my side, your side and the truth.

Anonymous

His argument is as thin as the
homeopathic soup that was made by
boiling the shadow of a pigeon that had
been starved to death.

Abraham Lincoln

I am not arguing with you –
I am telling you.

James McNeill Whistler,
The Gentle Art of Making Enemies

Ah, don't say that you agree with me.
When people agree with me I always feel
that I must be wrong.

Oscar Wilde, *The Critic as Artist* (essay)
and *Lady Windermere's Fan*

Attraction

She was short on intellect,
but long on shape.

George Ade

Mae:
How tall are you, son?

Man:
Ma-am, I'm six feet
seven inches.

Mae:
Let's forget the six feet
and talk about the
seven inches.

Mae West

Is that a gun in your
pocket or are you just
pleased to see me?

Mae West

Australians

God made the harbour, and that's all
right, but Satan made Sydney.

Anonymous (citizen of Sydney)

Australia is a huge rest home, where
no unwelcome news is ever wafted on
to the pages of the worst newspapers
in the world.

Germaine Greer

In Australia
Inter alia,
Mediocrities
Think they're Socrates.

Peter Porter

Bachelors

A bachelor is one who enjoys the chase but does not eat the game.

Anonymous

'Home, Sweet Home' must surely have been written by a bachelor.

Samuel Butler

A bachelor gets tangled up with a lot of women in order to avoid getting tied up by one.

Helen Rowland

Bachelors should be heavily taxed. It is not fair that some men should be happier than others.

Oscar Wilde

Baldness

A hair in the head is worth two in the brush.

Oliver Herford

He used to cut his hair, but now his hair has cut him.

Theodore Hook

There is more felicity on the far side of baldness than young men can possibly imagine.

Logan Pearsall Smith, *Afterthoughts*

Balding is God's way of showing you are only human ... he takes the hair off your head and sticks it in your ears.

Bruce Willis

Beards

Christlike in my behaviour,
Like every good believer,
I imitate the Saviour,
And cultivate a beaver.

Aldous Huxley, *Antic Hay*

There was an old man with a beard,
Who said, 'It is just as I feared!
Two Owls and a Hen,
Four Larks and a Wren
Have all built their
      nests in my beard.

Edward Lear,
A Book of Nonsense

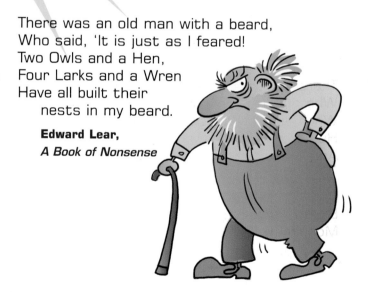

Bigamy

Spaulding:
Are we all going to get married?.

Teasdale:
... But that's bigamy.

Spaulding:
Yes, and it's bigame too.

Lines from film *Animal Crackers*.
Spoken by **Groucho Marx**

There was an old party of Lyme,
Who married three wives at one time.
When asked, 'Why the third?'
He replied, 'One's absurd,
And bigamy, sir, is a crime!'

William Cosmo Monkhouse

Bigamy is having one wife too many.
Monogamy is the same.

Oscar Wilde

13

Birth

If men bore the children, there would be only one born in each family.

Anonymous

Kath:
Can he be present at the birth of his child? ...

Ed:
It's all any reasonable child can expect if the dad is present at the conception.

Joe Orton, *Entertaining Mr Sloane*

Why is it that we rejoice at a birth and grieve at a funeral? It is because we are not the person involved.

Mark Twain, *Pudd'nhead Wilson*

On being chaffed for being an Irishman:

Because a man is born in a stable that does not make him a horse.

1st Duke of Wellington

When asked why he had been born in such an unfashionable place as Lowell, Massachusetts:

The explanation is quite simple. I wished to be near my mother.

James McNeill Whistler

Bitching

Oh, what a pretty dress – and so cheap!

Zsa Zsa Gabor

Tell me the history of that frock, Judy. It's obviously an old favourite. You were wise to remove the curtain rings.

Barry Humphries

When asked of Eleanor Roosevelt's whereabouts at a White House reception:

She's upstairs filing her teeth.

Groucho Marx

At the moment I am debarred from the pleasure of putting her in her place by the fact that she has not got one.

Edith Sitwell

Blondes

She was a brunette by birth but a blonde
by habit.

Arthur ('Bugs') Baer

It was a blonde. A blonde to make a
bishop kick a hole in a stained-glass
window.

Raymond Chandler, *Farewell, My Lovely*

She was a blonde – with a brunette past.

Gwyn Thomas

It's also possible that blondes prefer
gentlemen.

Mamie van Doren

Bores

Bore, n. A person who talks when you wish him to listen.

Ambrose Bierce, *The Cynic's Word Book*

Why can we remember the tiniest detail that has happened to us, and not remember how many times we have told it to the same persons?

François, Duc de La Rochefoucauld

On Sir Anthony Eden:

He was not only a bore; he bored for England.

Malcolm Muggeridge,
Tread Softly For You Tread on My Jokes

A bore is a man who, when you ask him how he is, tells you.

Bert Leston Taylor, *The So-Called Human Race*

Bottoms

I do most of my work sitting down; that's
where I shine.

Robert Benchley

The woman had a bottom of good sense.

Samuel Johnson

Au plus élevé trône du monde, si ne
sommes assis que sur notre cul

[Perched on the loftiest throne in the
world, we are still sitting on our behind].

Michel de Montaigne, *Essais*

Boys and girls

I like a girly girl, a womanly woman and a manly man, but I cannot abide a boyly boy.

Anonymous

You can take a boy out of the country but you can't take the country out of the boy.

Arthur ('Bugs') Baer

I am fond of children (except boys).

Lewis Carroll

Little boys should be obscene and not heard.

Oscar Wilde

Brains

He's very clever, but sometimes his
brains go to his head.

Margot Asquith

I have finally come to the conclusion
that a good reliable set of bowels is
worth more to a man than any quantity
of brains.

Josh Billings

The brain is a wonderful organ. It starts
working the moment you get up in the
morning, and does not stop until you get
into the office.

Robert Frost

Canadians

You have to know a man awfully well in Canada to know his surname.

John Buchan

I don't even know what street Canada is on.

Al Capone

Canada is a country so square that even the female impersonators are women.

Line from film *Outrageous!*

'I'm world-famous,' Dr Parks said, 'all over Canada.'

Mordecai Richler, *The Incomparable Auk*

Cats

The thing that astonished
him was that cats
should have two holes
cut in their coat,
exactly at the place
where their eyes are.

**George Christoph
Lichtenberg**

To a friend who was
upset t having to get rid
of his cat:

Have you tried curiosity?

Dorothy Parker

To whom none ever said scat,
No worthier cat
Ever sat on a mat
Or caught a rat:
Requies – cat.

John Greenleaf Whittier

Charity

It is better to give than to lend, and it costs about the same.

Philip Gibbs

If you pick up a starving dog and make him prosperous, he will not bite you. This is the principal difference between a dog and a man.

Mark Twain, *Pudd'nhead Wilson*

Simple rules for saving money: To save half, when you are fired by an eager impulse to contribute to charity, wait, and count to forty. To save three-quarters, count to sixty. To save it all, count to sixty-five.

Mark Twain, *Following the Equator*

Chastity

Da mihi castitatem et continentiam, sed
noli modo

[Give me chastity and continence – but
not yet].

Augustine of Hippo, *Confessions*

Chastity: the most unnatural of the
sexual perversions.

Aldous Huxley, *Eyeless in Gaza*

I may not be exactly what some people
consider a virgin, but I've been chaste.
Chased by every man.

Line from film *I Am a Camera*.
Spoken by **Julie Harris**

Children

It was no wonder that people were so horrible when they started life as children.

Kingsley Amis, *One Fat Englishman*

When asked whether he liked children:
Boiled or fried?

W.C. Fields

Ah, the patter of little feet around the house. There's nothing like having a midget for a butler.

W.C. Fields

I love children, especially when they cry, for then someone takes them away.

Nancy Mitford, *The Water Beetle*

A woman who thought herself to be a fine physical specimen once approached George Bernard Shaw suggesting that they combine to make a baby, saying: 'You have the greatest brain in the world and I have the most beautiful body; so we ought to produce the most perfect child.' He replied:

What if the child inherits my beauty and your brains?

George Bernard Shaw

Parents are the bones on which children sharpen their teeth.

Peter Ustinov

Cleanliness

Arthur:
I'm going to take a bath.
Hobson (butler):
I'll alert the media.

Line from film *Arthur*.
Spoken by **Dudley Moore**

Cleanliness is almost as bad as godliness.

Samuel Butler

If only he'd wash his neck, I'd wring it.

John Sparrow

Clothes

The sense of being well-dressed gives a
feeling of inward tranquility which religion
is powerless to bestow.

Miss C.F. Forbes

Only men who are not interested in
women are interested in women's clothes;
men who like women never notice what
they wear.

Anatole France

Clothes make the man. Naked people have
little or no influence in society.

Mark Twain

Compliments

Why, you're one of the most beautiful women I've ever seen, and that's not saying much for you.

> Line from film *Animal Crackers*.
> Spoken by **Groucho Marx**

Mrs Teasdale (gushingly):
Oh, your Excellency!

Firefly:
You're not so bad yourself.

> Lines from film *Duck Soup*.
> Spoken by **Groucho Marx**

I am leaving tonight;
Hannah and the rest
of the heavy baggage
will follow later.

5th Earl of Rosebery

Computers

To err is human but to really foul things up requires a computer.

Anonymous

We used to have lots of questions to which there were no answers. Now, with the computer, there are lots of answers to which we haven't thought up the questions.

Peter Ustinov

Conception

When a brigadier in the Indian Army asked his servant why, although many years married, he had had no children, the servant replied:

Ah, my wife, sir: she's inconceivable and impregnable.

Anonymous

Oh, what a tangled web we weave when first we practise to conceive.

Don Herold

In the early 1960s, Dr Edith Summerskill took part in an Oxford Union debate on contraception and abortion. Her opening words were:

Mr President, I cannot conceive ...

Edith Summerskill

Conscience

Conscience: the inner voice which warns
us that somebody may be looking.

H.L. Mencken, *A Little Book in C Major*

An uneasy conscience is a hair in the
mouth.

Mark Twain

Good friends, good books and a sleepy
conscience: this is the ideal life.

Mark Twain

Conscience does make egoists of us all.

Oscar Wilde, *The Picture of Dorian Gray*

Contraception

A fast word about oral contraception.
I asked a girl to go to bed with me and she said 'no'.

Woody Allen, *Woody Allen Volume Two*
(album)

The best contraceptive is a glass of cold water: not before or after, but instead.

Anonymous

Contraceptives should be used on every conceivable occasion.

Spike Milligan, *The Last Goon Show of All*
(BBC Radio show)

Cooking

There is one thing more exasperating than a wife who can cook and won't, and that's the wife who can't cook and will.

Robert Frost

I thought my mother was a bad cook but at least her gravy used to move about a bit.

Line from BBC Radio *Hancock's Half Hour*. Spoken by **Tony Hancock**

She did not so much cook as assassinate food.

Storm Jameson

The cook was a good cook, as cooks go; and as cooks go she went.

Saki, *Reginald*

Countryside

I am at two with nature.

Woody Allen

Country life is very good; in fact, the best – for cattle.

Sydney Smith

Anybody can be good in the country. There are no temptations there. That is the reason why people who live out of town are so uncivilised.

Oscar Wilde, *The Picture of Dorian Gray*

I see a little time in the country makes a man turn wild and unsociable, and only fit to converse with his horses, dogs, and his herds.

William Wycherley, *The Country Wife*

Courtship

Have the florist send some roses to Mrs Upjohn and write 'Emily I love you' on the back of the bill.

Line from film *A Day At the Races*.
Spoken by **Groucho Marx**

Courtship is to marriage, as a very witty prologue to a very dull play.

William Congreve, *The Old Bachelor*

A man in love is incomplete until he has married. Then he's finished.

Zsa Zsa Gabor

Cricket

On women playing cricket:

It's a bit like watching men knitting.

Len Hutton

Cricket – a game which the English, not being a spiritual people, have invented in order to give themselves a conception of eternity.

Lord Mancroft, *Bees in Some Bonnets*

Personally, I have always looked on cricket as organized loafing.

William Temple

Cynics

Cynic: a blackguard whose faulty vision
sees things as they are, not as they
ought to be.

Ambrose Bierce, *The Cynic's Word Book*

A cynic is what an idealist calls a realist.

Antony Jay and **Jonathan Lynn**

A cynic is a man who looks at the world
with a monocle in his mind's eye.

Carolyn Wells

A man who knows the price of everything
and the value of nothing.

Oscar Wilde, *Lady Windermere's Fan*

Death

It's not that I'm afraid to die. I just don't want to be there when it happens.

Woody Allen, *Death*

Death is nature's way of telling you to slow down.

Anonymous

Many people's tombstones should read, 'Died at 30. Buried at 60.'

Nicholas Murray Butler

You live and learn … then you die and forget it all.

Noël Coward

I have never wanted to see anybody die, but there are a few obituary notices I have read with pleasure.

Clarence Darrow

Once you're dead, you're made for life.

Jimi Hendrix

Death is a very dull, dreary affair. And my advice to you is to have nothing whatsoever to do with it.

W. Somerset Maugham

Since we have to speak well of the dead, let's knock them while they're alive.

John Sloan

Let us endeavour so to live that when we come to die even the undertaker will be sorry.

Mark Twain, *Pudd'nhead Wilson*

Democracy

Democracy: in which you say what you like and do what you're told.

Gerald Barry

The best argument against democracy is a five-minute conversation with the average voter.

Winston S. Churchill

Democracy substitutes election by the incompetent many for appointment by the corrupt few.

George Bernard Shaw,
Man and Superman

Democracy means simply the bludgeoning of the people by the people for the people.

Oscar Wilde, *The Soul of Man Under Socialism*
(essay)

Desires

The other day we had a long discourse
with [Lady Orkney] about love; and she
told us a saying ... which I thought
excellent, that in men, desire begets love,
and in women that love begets desire.

Jonathan Swift, *Journal to Stella*

In this world there are only two tragedies.
One is not getting what one wants, and
the other is getting it.

Oscar Wilde, *Lady Windermere's Fan*

Diets

She used to diet on any kind of food she could lay her hands on.

Arthur ('Bugs') Baer

Having taken it into his head not to eat vegetables, Brummell was asked by a lady if he had never eaten any at all in his life:

Yes, madam, I once ate a pea.

Beau Brummell

In the matter of diet – I have been persistently strict in sticking to the things that didn't agree with me until one or the other of us got the best of it.

Mark Twain

Disappointment

Nothing is so good as it seems
beforehand.

George Eliot, *Silas Marner*

When asked how he felt after a defeat in the
New York elections:

Somewhat like that boy in Kentucky, who
stubbed his toe while running to see his
sweetheart. The boy said he was too big
to cry, and far too badly hurt to laugh.

Abraham Lincoln

Blessed is the man who expects nothing,
for he shall never be disappointed.

Alexander Pope

Divorce

It was partially my fault that we got divorced ... I tended to place my wife under a pedestal.

Woody Allen

Alimony is the screwing you get for the screwing you got.

Anonymous

Divorces are made in heaven.

Oscar Wilde, *The Importance of Being Earnest*

Dogs

To Laurence Olivier's five-year-old daughter,
Tamsin, when she asked what two dogs were
doing together:

The doggie in front has suddenly gone
blind, and the other one has very kindly
offered to push him all the way to St
Dunstan's.

Noël Coward

I loathe people who keep dogs. They're
cowards who have not got the guts to
bite people themselves.

August Strindberg

If you want a friend, get a dog.

Line from film *Wall Street*.
Spoken by **Michael Douglas**

Drinking

'I love a Martini,' said Mabel,
'I only have two at the most.
After three, I am under
    the table,
After four, I am under
    my host.'

Anonymous

When asked how often he drank:

Only twice a day – when I'm
thirsty and when I'm not.

Brendan Behan

To Bessie Braddock MP, who had told him he
was drunk:

And you, madam, are ugly. But I shall be
sober in the morning.

Winston S. Churchill

I have taken more out of alcohol than
alcohol has taken out of me.

Winston S. Churchill

I was in love with a beautiful blonde once, dear. She drove me to drink. That's the one thing I'm indebted to her for.

> Line from film *Never Give a Sucker an Even Break*.
> Spoken by **W.C. Fields**

I exercise strong self-control. I never drink anything stronger than gin before breakfast.

W.C. Fields

I only drink to make other people seem more interesting.

George Jean Nathan

An alcoholic is someone you don't like who drinks as much as you do.

Dylan Thomas

I don't have a drink problem except when I can't get one.

Tom Waits

Dying words

Die, my dear doctor? That's the last thing I shall do.

Lord Palmerston

Last words before being shot by a sniper at the Battle of Spotsylvania in the American Civil War:

They couldn't hit an elephant at this dist–.

John Sedgwick

This wallpaper'll be the death of me – one of us'll have to go.

Oscar Wilde

No one on his deathbed ever said, 'I wish I had spent more time on my business.'

Arnold Zack

Education

'That's the reason they're called
lessons,' the Gryphon remarked:
'because they lessen from day to day.'

Lewis Carroll, *Alice's Adventures in
Wonderland*

How do you explain school to a higher
intelligence?

Line from film *E.T. The Extra-Terrestrial.*
Spoken by **Henry Thomas (Elliot)**

Education is what survives when what
has been learned has been forgotten.

B.F. Skinner

I never let my schooling interfere with
my education.

Mark Twain

Ego

That favourite subject, Myself.

James Boswell

Oscar Wilde:
When you and I are together, we never talk about anything except ourselves.

Whistler:
No, no, Oscar, you forget – when you and I are together, we never talk about anything except me.

James McNeill Whistler,
The Gentle Art of Making Enemies

Elections

Don't vote. The Government will get in.

Anonymous

Don't vote. You'll only encourage them.

Anonymous

The trouble with free elections is, you never know who is going to win.

Leonid Brezhnev

I just received the following wire from my generous Daddy – 'Dear Jack. Don't buy a single vote more than is necessary. I'll be damned if I'm going to pay for a landslide.'

John F. Kennedy

Enemies

On being told that another Labourite was 'his own worst enemy', Bevin replied:

Not while I'm alive, he ain't.

Ernest Bevin

Beware of meat twice boil'd, and an old foe reconciled.

Benjamin Franklin, *Poor Richard's Almanack*

Nobody ever fergits where he buried a hatchet.

Frank McKinney ('Kin') Hubbard,
Abe Martin's Broadcast

Next to having a staunch friend is the pleasure of having a brilliant enemy.

Oscar Wilde

Engagements

An engagement should come on a young
girl as a surprise, pleasant or unpleasant,
as the case may be.

Oscar Wilde, *The Importance of Being Earnest*

I am not in favour of long engagements.
They give people the opportunity of finding
out each other's characters before
marriage, which I think is never advisable.

Oscar Wilde, *The Importance of Being Earnest*

An engagement is hardly a serious one
that has not been broken off at least
once.

Oscar Wilde

The English

Englishmen hate two things – racial discrimination and Irishmen.

Anonymous (Irishman)

Most Englishmen can never get over the embarrassing fact that they were born in bed with a woman.

Anonymous (Scotsman)

They tell me that the English are a people who travel all over the world to laugh at other people.

Anonymous (Spaniard)

In Bangkok at twelve o'clock
They foam at the mouth and run.
But mad dogs and Englishmen
Go out in the mid-day sun.

Noël Coward, *Mad Dogs and Englishmen*
(song)

If an Englishman gets run down by a
truck, he apologises to the truck.

Jackie Mason

An Englishman, even if he is alone, forms
an orderly queue of one.

George Mikes, *How To Be An Alien*

An Englishman thinks he is moral when
he is only uncomfortable.

George Bernard Shaw, *Man and Superman*

Exams

... I should have liked to be asked to say what I knew. They always tried to ask what I did not know.

Winston S. Churchill, *My Early Life*

In an examination those who do not wish to know ask questions of those who cannot tell.

Walter Raleigh, *Laughter from a Cloud*

Do not on any account attempt to write on both sides of the paper at once.

W.C. Sellar and **R.J. Yeatman,**
1066 and All That

In examinations the foolish ask questions that the wise cannot answer.

Oscar Wilde

xcuses

I'd like to kiss you, but I just washed my hair. Bye!

> Line from film *Cabin in the Cotton*.
> Spoken by **Bette Davis**

Tell him I've been too f***ing busy – or vice versa.

> **Dorothy Parker**

Asked by Harold Ross, editor of The New Yorker, why she hadn't been in to the office during the week to write her piece:

Someone was using the pencil.

> **Dorothy Parker**

On why snow had disrupted rail services, even though a big chill had been correctly forecast:

It was the wrong kind of snow.

> **Terry Worrall, British Rail's director of operations**

Exercise

Exercise is the most *awful* illusion.
The secret is a lot of aspirin and
marrons glacés.

Noël Coward

Exercise is bunk. If you are healthy, you
don't need it. If you are sick, you shouldn't
take it.

Henry Ford

I take my only exercise acting as
pallbearer at the funerals of my friends
who exercise regularly.

Mark Twain

I am pushing sixty. That is enough
exercise for me.

Mark Twain

xperience

You should make a point of trying every experience once, excepting incest and folk-dancing.

Anonymous

Experience is a revelation in the light of which we renounce our errors of youth for those of age.

Ambrose Bierce

The only thing that experience teaches us is that experience teaches us nothing.

André Maurois

Experience was of no ethical value. It was merely the name men gave to their mistakes.

Oscar Wilde, *The Picture of Dorian Gray*

He is old enough to know worse.

Oscar Wilde

Faces

Her face was her chaperone.

Rupert Hughes

I never forget a face, but in your case I'll be glad to make an exception.

Groucho Marx

At 50, everyone has the face he deserves.

George Orwell

A dowdy dull girl, with one of those characteristic British faces that, once seen, are never remembered.

Oscar Wilde, *The Picture of Dorian Gray*

Failures

Failure has gone to his head.

Wilson Mizner

There are interesting failures. There are prestige failures, and there are financial failures, but this is the sort of failure that gives failures a bad name.

Line from film *Please Don't Eat the Daisies*.
Spoken by **David Niven**

I haven't had a hit film since Joan Collins was a virgin.

Burt Reynolds

Faithfulness

Those who are faithful know only the trivial side of love: it is the faithless who know love's tragedies.

Oscar Wilde, *The Picture of Dorian Gray*

Faithfulness is to the emotional life what consistency is to the life of the intellect, simply a confession of failure.

Oscar Wilde, *The Picture of Dorian Gray*

Young men want to be faithful and are not; old men want to be faithless and are not.

Oscar Wilde, *The Picture of Dorian Gray*

Fame

A test of whether you have achieved true fame is when a deranged person believes himself to be you.

Anonymous

Fame is failure disguised as money.

Brendan Behan

In short, whoever you may be,
To this conclusion you'll agree,
When everyone is somebodee,
Then no one's anybody.

W.S. Gilbert, *The Gondoliers*

Families

Where does the family start? It starts with a young man falling in love with a girl – no superior alternative has yet been found.

Winston S. Churchill

To the family – that dear octopus from whose tentacles we never quite escape nor, in our inmost hearts, ever quite wish to.

Dodie Smith, *Dear Octopus*

A family is a terrible encumbrance, especially when one is not married.

Oscar Wilde, *Vera: Or The Nihilists*

Fashion

Fashion is what one wears oneself.
What is unfashionable is what other
people wear.

Oscar Wilde, *An Ideal Husband*

Women's styles may change but their
designs remain the same.

Oscar Wilde

After all, what is a fashion? From the
artistic point of view, it is usually a form
of ugliness so intolerable that we have
to alter it every six months.

Oscar Wilde

Fathers

I wish either my father or my mother, or indeed both of them, as they were in duty both equally bound to it, had minded what they were about when they begot me.

Laurence Sterne, *Tristram Shandy*

When I was a boy of fourteen, my father was so ignorant I could hardly stand to have the old man around. But when I got to be twenty-one, I was astonished at how much he had learned in seven years.

Mark Twain

Fathers should be neither seen nor heard. That is the only proper basis for family life.

Oscar Wilde, *An Ideal Husband*

Fatness

Imprisoned in every fat man a thin one is wildly signalling to be let out.

Cyril Connolly, *The Unquiet Grave*

Alfred Hitchcock:
One look at you, Mr Shaw, and I know there's famine in the land.

George Bernard Shaw:
One look at you, Mr Hitchcock, and I know who caused it.

George Bernard Shaw

The Right Hon was a tubby little chap who looked as if he had been poured into his clothes and had forgotten to say 'When!'

P.G. Wodehouse, *Very Good, Jeeves*

Faults

Si nous n'avions point de défauts, nous ne prendrions pas tant de plaisir à en remarquer dans les autres

[If we had no faults, we should not take so much pleasure in remarking them in others].

François, Duc de La Rochefoucauld, *Maximes*

Don't tell your friends their social faults; they will cure the fault and never forgive you.

Logan Pearsall Smith, *All Trivia*

Always acknowledge a fault frankly. This will throw those in authority off their guard and give you opportunity to commit more.

Mark Twain

Feminism

I was the first woman to
burn my bra – it took the fire
department four days to put
it out.

Dolly Parton

We are
becoming
the men we
wanted to
marry.

Gloria Steinem

I myself have never been able to find out
precisely what feminism is: I only know
that people call me a feminist whenever
I express sentiments that differentiate
me from a doormat or a prostitute.

Rebecca West

Fishing

I never lost a little fish. Yes, I am free to say, It always was the biggest fish I caught that got away.

Eugene Field

There are more fish taken out of a stream than ever were in it.

Oliver Herford

Fly fishing may be a very pleasant amusement; but angling or float fishing I can only compare to a stick and a string, with a worm at one end and a fool at the other.

Samuel Johnson

lattery

Won't you come into the garden? I would like my roses to see you.

Richard Brinsley Sheridan

I suppose flattery hurts no one – that is, if he doesn't inhale.

Adlai Stevenson

'Tis an old maxim in the schools,
That Vanity's the food of fools;
Yet now and then your men of wit
Will condescend to taste a bit.

Jonathan Swift, *Cadenus and Vanessa*

Flirting

Flirt: a woman who thinks it's every man for herself.

Anonymous

Tell me about yourself – your struggles, your dreams, your telephone number.

Peter Arno

Nothing sharpens the wits like promiscuous flirtation.

George Moore

To George Bernard Shaw after an empty flirtation (1887):

You had no right to write the Preface if you were not going to write the book.

E. Nesbit

Food

There is no such thing as a little garlic.

Arthur ('Bugs') Baer

Eat to live, and not live to eat.

Benjamin Franklin,
Poor Richard's Almanack

Parsley
Is gharsely.

Ogden Nash,
Good Intentions

He was a bold
man that first
eat an oyster.

Jonathan Swift, *Polite Conversation*

After a good dinner, one can forgive
anybody, even one's own relations.

Oscar Wilde, *A Woman of No Importance*

Fools

It is better to be silent and be thought
a fool than to speak out and remove all
doubt.

Anonymous

Fools' names, like fools' faces,
Are often seen in public places.

Anonymous

When he said we were trying to make a
fool of him, I could only murmur that the
Creator had beat us to it.

Ilka Chase

To a tiresome escort who exclaimed, 'I can't
bear fools':

That's queer. Your mother could.

Dorothy Parker

Football

He is not fit to lace George Best's drinks.

John Roberts

The first ninety minutes are the most
important.

Bobby Robson

Some people think football is a matter of
life and death. I don't like that attitude.
I can assure them it is much more
serious than that.

Bill Shankly

Forgetfulness

One always forgets the most important things. It's the things that one can't remember that stay with you.

Alan Bennett, *Forty Years On*

'It's a poor sort of memory that only works backwards,' the Queen remarked.

Lewis Carroll, *Through the Looking-Glass and What Alice Found There*

There are three things I always forget. Names, faces, and – the third I can't remember.

Italo Svevo

The French

If it were not for the government, we should have nothing left to laugh at in France.

Nicolas-Sébastien Chamfort

Comment voulez-vous gouverner un pays qui a deux cent quarante-six variétés de fromage?

[How can you govern a country which produces 246 different kinds of cheese?].

Charles de Gaulle

France is a country where the money falls apart in your hands and you can't tear the toilet paper.

Billy Wilder

Friends

God protect me from my friends.

Anonymous

The feeling of friendship is like that of
being comfortably filled
with roast beef; love,
like being enlivened with
champagne.

> **James Boswell,**
> *The Life of Samuel Johnson*

There is no spectacle
more agreeable than
to observe an
old friend fall
from a roof-top.

Confucius

A friend that ain't in
need is a friend indeed.

Frank McKinney ('Kin') Hubbard

That is just the way of the world; an
enemy can partly ruin a man, but it takes
a good-natured injudicious friend to
complete the thing and make it perfect.

Mark Twain, *Pudd'nhead Wilson*

The proper office of a friend is to side with
you when you are in the wrong. Nearly
everybody will side with you when you are
in the right.

Mark Twain

Whenever a friend succeeds, a little
something in me dies.

Gore Vidal

Friendship is far more tragic than love.
It lasts longer.

Oscar Wilde

Gambling

Horse sense is a good judgement which keeps horses from betting on people.

W.C. Fields

When a gambler asks Cuthbert J. Twillie, 'Is this a game of chance?':

Not the way I play it.

Line from film *My Little Chickadee*.
Spoken by **W.C. Fields**

The race is not always to the swift nor the battle to the strong, but that's the way to bet.

Damon Runyon

Gardening

Oh, Adam was a gardener, and God who
  made him sees
That half a proper gardener's work is done
  upon the knees.

Rudyard Kipling, *The Glory of the Garden*
(poem)

A garden is a lovesome thing? What rot!

J.A. Lindon, *My Garden with a stern look at
T.E. Brown* (poem)

I have nothing against gardening. I just
prefer not to be there when it happens.

Tracey Macleod

Genius

Genius is one per cent inspiration and
ninety-nine per cent perspiration.

Thomas Alva Edison

Genius is the talent of a man who is dead.

Edmond de Goncourt

When a true genius appears in the world,
you may know him by this sign, that the
dunces are all in confederacy against him.

Jonathan Swift, *Thoughts on Various Subjects*

At the New York Custom House, on arriving in
the United States (1882) and asked by the
customs officer if he had anything to declare:

I have nothing to declare except my
genius.

Oscar Wilde

Gentlemen

Definition of an English gentleman:

Useful at a hunt ball. Invaluable in a shipwreck.

Anonymous

Gentlemen prefer blondes, but take what they can get.

Don Herold

The only infallible rule we know is, that the man who is always talking about being a gentleman never is one.

R.S. Surtees, *Ask Mamma*

A gentleman is one who never hurts anyone's feelings unintentionally.

Oscar Wilde

The Germans

The only way to treat a Prussian is to step on his toes until he apologizes.

Anonymous (Austrian proverb)

Springtime for Hitler and Germany,
Deutschland is happy and gay.
We're marching to a faster pace,
Look out, here comes the Master Race!

Lines from song in musical *Springtime for Hitler* from film **The Producers**

My philological studies have satisfied me that a gifted person ought to learn English (barring spelling and pronouncing) in thirty hours, French in thirty days, and German in thirty years.

Mark Twain

God

When God made man she was only testing.

Anonymous

I am ready to meet my Maker. Whether my Maker is ready for the ordeal of meeting me is another matter.

Winston S. Churchill

Forgive, O Lord, my little jokes on Thee
And I'll forgive Thy great big one on me.

Robert Frost,
Cluster of Faith
(poem)

I sometimes think that God in creating man somewhat overestimated his ability.

Oscar Wilde

87

Golf

[Golf is] cow-pasture pool.

O.K. Bovard

If I had my way no man guilty of golf would be eligible to any office of trust or profit under the United States.

H.L. Mencken, *Heathen Days*

Golf is a good walk spoiled.

Mark Twain

Goodness

The word 'good' has many meanings.
For example, if a man were to shoot his
grandmother at a range of five hundred
yards, I should call him a good shot, but
not *necessarily* a good man.

G.K. Chesterton

When I'm good, I'm very, very good. But
when I'm bad, I'm better.

Line from film *I'm No Angel*.
Spoken by **Mae West**

To be good is noble; but to show others
how to be good is nobler and no trouble.

Mark Twain, *Following the Equator*

No good deed goes unpunished.

Oscar Wilde

Gratitude

In speech accepting Oscar:

I just want to thank everyone I met in my entire life.

Kim Basinger

To a nun nursing him on his deathbed:

Thank you, Sister. May you be the mother of a bishop!

Brendan Behan

Of Marilyn Monroe:

Copulation was, I'm sure, Marilyn's uncomplicated way of saying thank you.

Nunnally Johnson

The gratitude of place-expectants is a lively sense of future favours.

Robert Walpole

Guests

It was a delightful visit; – perfect, in
being much too short.

Jane Austen, *Emma*

I'm a particularly loathsome guest and
I eat like a vulture. Unfortunately, the
resemblance doesn't end there.

Groucho Marx

In reply to hostess's inquiry whether he was
enjoying himself at party:

Certainly, there is nothing else here to
enjoy.

George Bernard Shaw

Yes, dear Frank [Harris], we believe you:
you have dined in every house in London,
once.

Oscar Wilde

Hair

What's the point of getting your hair cut?
It only grows again.

Alphonse Allais

Grey hair is a sign of age, not of wisdom.

Anonymous

When red-haired people are above a
certain social grade their hair is auburn.

Mark Twain

'And go and get
your hair cut,'
screamed Beatrice.
'You look like a
chrysanthemum.'

P.G. Wodehouse,
Hot Water

Happiness

Happiness? A good cigar, a good meal, and a good woman – or a bad woman. It depends on how much happiness you can handle.

George Burns

Leavin' me as happy as a dog with two tails.

Mark Twain, *The Adventures of Thomas Jefferson Snodgrass*

Happiness is no laughing matter.

Richard Whately, *Apothegms*

Some cause happiness wherever they go; others whenever they go.

Oscar Wilde

Health

I reckon being ill as one of the greatest pleasures of life, provided one is not too ill and is not obliged to work until one is better.

Samuel Butler, *The Way of All Flesh*

One of the minor pleasures in life is to be slightly ill.

Harold Nicolson

Early to rise and early to bed makes a male healthy and wealthy and dead.

James Thurber

eaven and Hell

Heaven protects children, sailors, and drunken men.

Anonymous

At any rate there will be no wedding presents in heaven.

Samuel Butler

There have been many definitions of hell, but for the English the best definition is that it is a place where the Germans are the police, the Swedish are the comedians, and the Italians are the defence force, Frenchmen dig the roads, the Belgians are the pop singers, the Spanish run the railways, the Turks cook the food, the Irish are the waiters, the Greeks run the government and the common language is Dutch.

David Frost and **Antony Jay,**
To England with Love

L'Enfer, c'est les Autres
[Hell is other people].

Jean-Paul Sartre, *Huis Clos*

On the existence of heaven and hell:
I don't want to express an opinion. You
see, I have friends in both places.

Mark Twain

Heaven for climate; hell for society.

Mark Twain

ome

Home is where the television is.

Anonymous

Be it ever so humbug, there's no place like home.

Noël Coward

Home is where you go to when you've nowhere to go.

Bette Davis

Home is the place where, when you have to go there, they have to take you in.

Robert Frost

Honesty

No man ever made more than a million dollars honestly.

Charles May Oelrichs

If you want to be thought a liar always tell the truth.

Logan Pearsall Smith

Honesty is the best policy, but it is not the cheapest.

Mark Twain

quips and
quotes

Husbands

Husbands are like fires. They go out when unattended.

Zsa Zsa Gabor

In answer to the question 'How many husbands have you had?':

You mean apart from my own?

Zsa Zsa Gabor

Do married men make the best husbands?

James Gibbons Huneker

American women expect to find in their husbands a perfection that English women only hope to find in their butlers.

W. Somerset Maugham

A husband is what is left of the lover after the nerve has been extracted.

Helen Rowland

I am, dear Prue, a little in drink, but at all times yr faithful husband.

Richard Steele

The husbands of very beautiful women belong to the criminal classes.

Oscar Wilde, *The Picture of Dorian Gray*

Idleness

Cultivated idleness seems to me to be
the proper occupation for man.

Oscar Wilde

Lady Bracknell:
Do you smoke?

Jack Worthing:
Well, yes, I must admit I smoke.

Lady Bracknell:
I am glad to hear it. A man should
always have an occupation of some kind.
There are far too many idle men in
London as it is.

Oscar Wilde,
The Importance of Being Earnest

Ignorance

Gross ignorance −144 times worse than ordinary ignorance.

Bennett Cerf, *The Laugh's on Me*

Even his ignorance is encyclopedic.

Stanislaw J. Lec, *Unkempt Thoughts*

Presently Mr Bixby turned on me and said: 'What is the name of the first point above New Orleans?' I was gratified to be able to answer promptly and I did. I said I didn't know.

Mark Twain, *Life on the Mississippi*

he Irish

Anyone who isn't confused here doesn't really understand what's going on.

Anonymous (Belfast citizen)

On the situation in Ulster, 1970s:

Ah, well, they say it's not as bad as they say it is.

Anonymous (Irish woman)

I believe they manage things better across the other side [in America]. Sure God help the Irish, if it was raining soup, they'd be out with forks.

Brendan Behan, *Brendan Behan's Island*

I said, 'It is most extraordinary weather for this time of year.' He replied, 'Ah, it isn't this time of year at all.'

Oliver St John Gogarty,
It Isn't This Time of Year at All

The Irish are a fair people; – they never speak well of one another.

Samuel Johnson

Ireland is a country in which the probable never happens and the impossible always does.

John Pentland Mahaffy

Put an Irishman on the spit, and you can always get another Irishman to turn him.

George Bernard Shaw

Kissing

I don't know how to kiss, or I would kiss
you. Where do the noses go?

> Line from film *For Whom the Bell Tolls*.
> Spoken by **Ingrid Bergman**

Being kissed by a man who *didn't* wax his
moustache was – like eating an egg
without salt.

> **Rudyard Kipling,**
> *The Story of
> the Gadsbys*

Kissing don't last:
cookery do!

> **George Meredith,**
> *The Ordeal of
> Richard Feverel*

Laughter

Laughter is the hiccup of a fool.

Anonymous

A merry heart doeth good like a medicine.

The Bible. Proverbs 17:22

The day most wholly lost is the one on which one does not laugh.

Nicholas-Sébastien Chamfort, *Maximes et pensées*

Quamquam ridentem dicere verum / Quid vetat?

[Why should one not speak the truth, laughing?].

Horace

Laugh and the world laughs with you Weep and you weep alone.

Ella Wheeler Wilcox, *Solitude* (poem)

The Law

The penalty for laughing in the courtroom is six months in jail: if it were not for this penalty, the jury would never hear the evidence.

H.L. Mencken

When a magistrate asked if he was trying to show contempt for the court:

No, I'm trying to conceal it.

Wilson Mizner

A lawyer with his briefcase can steal more than a thousand men with guns.

Mario Puzo, *The Godfather*

As scarce as lawyers in heaven.

Mark Twain, *The Celebrated Jumping Frog of Calaveras County*

Laws of life

When all else fails, read the instructions.

Anonymous ('Cahn's Axiom')

If anything can go wrong, it will.

Anonymous ('Murphy's Law')

Seven-eighths of everything can't be seen.

Anonymous ('Iceberg Theorem')

The easiest way to find something lost around the house is to buy a replacement.

Anonymous ('Rosenbaum's Law')

When all else fails – and the instructions are missing – kick it.

Anonymous

The more underdeveloped the country, the
more overdeveloped the women.

John Kenneth Galbraith

Anyone who says he isn't going to resign
four times, definitely will.

John Kenneth Galbraith

A shortcut is the longest distance
between two points.

Charles Issawi

If it works well, they'll stop making it.

Jane Otten and **Russell Baker**

It is impossible to make anything foolproof
because fools are so ingenious.

H.W. Robinson of Co. Down

Lies

Of a friend:

She tells enough white lies to ice a wedding cake.

Margot Asquith

A lie is an abomination unto the Lord and a very present help in time of trouble.

Adlai Stevenson

He was not a direct liar but he would subtly convey untruths.

Mark Twain

The only form of lying that is absolutely beyond reproach is lying for its own sake.

Oscar Wilde

Life

This is not a dress rehearsal, this is
real life.

Anonymous

Life ... is like a cup of tea; the more
heartily we drink, the sooner we reach
the dregs.

J.M. Barrie, *The Admirable Crichton*

My momma always said, life was like a
box of chocolates ... you never know
what you're gonna get.

Line from film *Forrest Gump*.
Spoken by **Tom Hanks**

Life doesn't imitate art. It imitates bad
television.

Line from film *Husbands and Wives*.
Spoken by **Woody Allen**

Laugh it off, laugh it off; it's all part of life's rich pageant.

Arthur Marshall

Life's a tough proposition, and the first hundred years are the hardest.

Wilson Mizner

Oh, isn't life a terrible thing, thank God?

Dylan Thomas, *Under Milk Wood* (radio play)

What a pity that in life we only get our lessons when they are of no use to us.

Oscar Wilde, *Lady Windermere's Fan*

Love

Love – the delightful interval between meeting a beautiful girl and discovering that she looks like a haddock.

John Barrymore

'Tis better to have loved and lost than never to have lost at all.

Samuel Butler,
The Way of All Flesh

Love is like the measles; we all have to go through it.

Jerome K. Jerome,
Idle Thoughts of an Idle Fellow

It is better to have loved a short man, than never to have loved a tall.

Miles Kington

Love is not the dying moan of a distant violin – it is the triumphant twang of a bedspring.

S.J. Perelman

If love is the answer could you rephrase the question?

Lily Tomlin

Men always want to be a woman's first love. We women have a more subtle instinct about things. What we like is to be a man's last romance.

Oscar Wilde, *A Woman of No Importance*

Make-up

Most women are not so young as they
are painted.

Max Beerbohm

She had a beautiful complexion when she
first came, but it faded out by degrees in
an unaccountable way. However, it is not
lost for good. I found the most of it on my
shoulder afterwards.

Mark Twain, *Sketches New and Old*

As long as a woman can look ten years
younger than her own daughter, she is
perfectly satisfied.

Oscar Wilde

Marriage

All marriages are happy. It's the living together afterward that causes all the trouble.

Anonymous

'What are you giving the bride and groom?'
Reply: 'Oh, about three months.'

Anonymous

In answer to question, Is it true that married people live longer?:

No, it just seems longer.

Line from film *The Bank Dick*.
Spoken by **W.C. Fields**

All tragedies are finish'd by death,
All comedies are ended by a marriage.

Lord Byron, *Don Juan* (poem)

Marriage is a wonderful invention; but, then again, so is a bicycle repair kit.

Billy Connolly

Marriage isn't a word … it's a sentence!

Line/screen title from silent film *The Crowd*

Never go to bed mad. Stay up and fight.

Phyllis Diller, *Phyllis Diller's Housekeeping Hints*

Marriage is a mistake every man should make.

George Jessel

To keep your marriage brimming
With love in the loving cup,
Whenever you're wrong, admit it,
Whenever you're right, shut up.

Ogden Nash, *A Word to Husbands* (poem)

Why fool around with hamburger when you have steak at home?

Paul Newman

It does not much signify whom one marries, as one is sure to find next morning that it is someone else.

Samuel Rogers

Marriage is popular because it combines the maximum of temptation with the maximum of opportunity.

George Bernard Shaw, *Man and Superman*

Marriage: a ceremony in which rings are put on the finger of the lady and through the nose of the gentleman.

Herbert Spencer

Will you take this woman Matti Richards
... to be your awful wedded wife?

Dylan Thomas, *Under Milk Wood* (radio play)

Love seems the swiftest but it is the
slowest of all growths. No man or woman
really knows what perfect love is until
they have been married for a quarter of
a century.

Mark Twain

Marriage is a great institution, but I'm
not ready for an institution yet.

Mae West

Meanness

In reply to robber demanding 'Your money or your life!':

I'm thinking it over.

Jack Benny

In reply to advertising slogan 'If — — Offered You A Cigarette, It Would Be A De Reszke':

If Godfrey Winn offered you a cigarette ... it would be a bloody miracle!

Noël Coward

On Bing Crosby:

If he can't take it with him, he's not going.

Bob Hope

Men

Women's faults are many
Men have only two:
Everything they say
And everything they do.

Anonymous

If they can put a man on the moon, why
don't they put them all there?

Anonymous

I married beneath
me. All women do.

Nancy Astor

Men are those
creatures with
two legs and eight hands.

Jayne Mansfield

Men have a much better time of it than women; for one thing, they marry later; for another thing, they die earlier.

H.L. Mencken, *A Mencken Chrestomathy*

The more I see of men, the more I like dogs.

Madame Roland

It's not the men in my life, but the life in my men.

Mae West

A hard man is good to find.

Mae West

Middle age

Middle age occurs when you are too young
to take up golf and too old to rush up to
the net.

Franklin P. Adams

The really frightening thing about middle age
is the knowledge that you'll grow out of it.

Doris Day

Boys will be boys, and so will a lot of
middle-aged men.

Frank McKinney ('Kin') Hubbard

I wouldn't mind being called middle-aged if
only I knew a few more 100-year-old people.

Dean Martin

Middle age is when, wherever you go on
holiday, you pack a sweater.

Denis Norden

Misfortunes

Misfortunes and twins never come singly.

'Josh Billings' (Henry Wheeler Shaw)

Asked to define the difference between a calamity and a misfortune:

If, for instance, Mr Gladstone were to fall into the river, that would be a misfortune. But if anyone were to pull him out, that would be a calamity.

Benjamin Disraeli

Ay, people are generally calm at the misfortunes of others.

Oliver Goldsmith, *She Stoops to Conquer*

Mistakes

I have made mistakes, but I have never
made the mistake of claiming that I never
made one.

James Gordon Bennett II

The man who makes no mistakes does not
usually make anything.

Edward John Phelps

Nowadays most people die of a sort of
creeping common sense, and discover,
when it is too late, that the only thing
one never regrets are one's mistakes.

Oscar Wilde, *The Picture of Dorian Gray*

Modesty

The English instinctively admire any man who has no talent and is modest about it.

James Agate, *Ego 9*

Modesty is the only sure bait when you angle for praise.

4th Earl of Chesterfield

I have often wished I had time to cultivate modesty ... But I am too busy thinking about myself.

Edith Sitwell

I was born modest, but it didn't last.

Mark Twain

Money

Money can't buy you happiness but you can be miserable in comfort.

Anonymous

There are no pockets in shrouds.

Anonymous

If you would know the value of Money, go and borrow some.

Benjamin Franklin, *Poor Richard's Almanack*

You Can't Take It With You.

Moss Hart and **George S. Kaufman**

The safest way to double your money is to fold it over once and put it in your pocket.

Frank McKinney ('Kin') Hubbard

Money can't buy friends, but you can get a better class of enemy.

Spike Milligan, *Puckoon*

Money talks, they say. All it ever said to me was 'goodbye'.

Line from film ***None But the Lonely Heart***. Spoken by **Cary Grant**

Asked in old age why he persisted in robbing banks:

Because that's where the money is.

Willie Sutton

When I was young I used to think that money was the most important thing in life; now that I am old, I know that it is.

Oscar Wilde

Mothers

Who took me from my bed so hot
And placed me shivering on the pot,
Nor asked me whether I would or not?
My Mother!

Anonymous

All women dress like their mothers, that
is their tragedy. No man ever does. That
is his.

Alan Bennett, *Forty Years On.*
Compare Wilde below

Algernon:
All women become like their mothers. That
is their tragedy. No man does. That's his.

Oscar Wilde, *The Importance of Being Earnest*

Mothers-in-law

Peter remained on friendly terms with Christ notwithstanding Christ's having healed his mother-in-law.

Samuel Butler

My mother-in-law has come round to our house at Christmas seven years running. This year we're having a change. We're going to let her in.

Les Dawson

I just came from a pleasure trip: I took my mother-in-law to the airport.

Henny Youngman

Motorists

To Daisy, when she blames her car for
an accident:

Mama, cars don't behave. They are
behaved upon.

> Line from film *Driving Miss Daisy*.
> Spoken by **Dan Aykroyd**

God would not have invented the
automobile if he had intended me to walk.

> **J.E. Morpurgo,** *The Road to Athens*

There are a number of mechanical devices
which increase sexual arousal, particularly
in women. Chief among these is the
Mercedes 380SL convertible.

> **P.J. O'Rourke,** *Modern Manners*

It is the overtakers who keep the
undertakers busy.

> **William Pitts**

Nakedness

On David Storey's play *The Changing Room*, which included a male nude scene:

I didn't pay three pounds fifty just to see half a dozen acorns and a chipolata.

Noël Coward

When asked if she had really posed for a 1947 calendar with nothing on:

I had the radio on.

Marilyn Monroe

On being asked what she wore in bed:

Chanel No. 5.

Marilyn Monroe

Neighbours

Mr Bennet speaking:

For what do we live, but to make sport for our neighbours, and laugh at them in our turn?

Jane Austen, *Pride and Prejudice*

It is an offence to have a wireless on too loud these still summer evenings. It can annoy your neighbour. An even better way is to throw a dead cat on the lawn ...

Ronald Fletcher

Philosophy may teach us to bear with equanimity the misfortunes of our neighbours.

Oscar Wilde

Old age

I got used to my arthritis
To my dentures I'm resigned,
I can manage my bifocals,
But Lord I miss my mind.

Anonymous

I will never be an old man. To me, old age
is always fifteen years older than I am.

Bernard Baruch

Old age is the outpatients' department
of Purgatory.

Hugh Cecil

Old age isn't so bad when you consider
the alternative.

Maurice Chevalier

The older I grow, the more I distrust the familiar doctrine that age brings wisdom.

H.L. Mencken

Growing old is like being increasingly penalized for a crime you haven't committed.

Anthony Powell, *Temporary Kings*

Every man desires to live long but no man would be old.

Jonathan Swift, *Thoughts on Various Subjects*

The old should neither be seen nor heard.

Oscar Wilde

Optimism

The optimist proclaims that we live in the best of all possible worlds; and the pessimist fears this is true.

James Branch Cabell, *The Silver Stallion*

An optimist is a girl who mistakes a bulge for a curve.

Ring Lardner

Cheer up! The worst is yet to come.

Mark Twain

I'm an optimist, but I'm an optimist who takes his raincoat.

Harold Wilson

Orgasms

In the case of some women, orgasms take quite a bit of time. Before signing on with such a partner, make sure you are willing to lay aside, say, the month of June, with sandwiches having to be brought in.

Bruce Jay Friedman

Girl at party:

I finally had an orgasm ... and my doctor told me it was the *wrong* kind.

Line from film *Manhattan*

Now I know what I've been faking all these years.

Line from film *Private Benjamin*.
Spoken by **Goldie Hawn**

Paranoia

I wouldn't be paranoid if people didn't pick on me.

Anonymous

Just because you're paranoid, it doesn't mean they're not out to get you.

Anonymous

Even a paranoid can have enemies.

Henry Kissinger

Margaret said: 'Has it ever struck you that when people get persecution mania, they usually have a good deal to feel persecuted about?'

C.P. Snow, *The Affair*

Parents

Some people seem compelled by unkind
fate to parental servitude for life. There is
no form of penal servitude much worse
than this.

Samuel Butler

'Why'd you have me if you didn't want me?'

'Who knew it would be you?'

Joseph Heller, *Good as Gold*

Mom and Pop were just a couple of kids
when they got married. He was eighteen,
she was sixteen, and I was three.

Billie Holiday, *Lady Sings the Blues*

The question of who are the best people to take charge of children is a very difficult one; but it is quite certain that the parents are the very worst.

William Morris

Before I got married I had six theories about bringing up children; and now I have six children, and no theories.

2nd Earl of Rochester

Children begin by loving their parents; after a time they judge them. Rarely, if ever, do they forgive them.

Oscar Wilde, *A Woman of No Importance*

Pessimists

A pessimist is one who has been
intimately acquainted with an optimist.

Elbert Hubbard,
A Thousand and One Epigrams

There is no sadder sight than a young
pessimist, except an old optimist.

Mark Twain

Pessimist: one who, when he has the
choice of two evils, chooses both.

Oscar Wilde

Politicians

A politician is an animal who can sit on a fence and yet keep both ears to the ground.

Anonymous

A politician is a person who approaches every subject with an open mouth.

Anonymous

A politician is an arse upon which everyone has sat except a man.

e.e. cummings

Politicians are the same all over. They promise to build a bridge even when there is no river.

Nikita Khruschev

He was the consummate politician. He
didn't lie, neither did he tell the truth.

John Lundberg

He knows nothing and he thinks he knows
everything. That points clearly to a
political career.

George Bernard Shaw, *Major Barbara*

The country is going down the drain and
they are squabbling about the size of the
plughole.

Jeremy Thorpe

The only definition of an honest politician
is one who once bought stays bought.

Mark Twain

Promiscuity

Good girls to go heaven, bad girls go everywhere.

Helen Gurley Brown

What is a promiscuous person? It's usually someone who is getting more sex than you are.

Victor Lownes

There's a lot of promiscuity around these days and I'm all for it.

Ben Travers

So many men, so little time!

Mae West

She's been on more laps than a napkin.

Walter Winchell

Punctuality

When criticized for continually arriving late for
work in the City in 1919:

But think how early I go.

Lord Castlerosse

The only way of catching a train I ever
discovered is to miss the train before.

G.K. Chesterton

I've been on a calendar, but never on time.

Marilyn Monroe

He was always late on principle, his
principle being that punctuality is the thief
of time.

Oscar Wilde, *The Picture of Dorian Gray*

Purity

I knew a girl who was so pure
She couldn't say the word Manure.

Reginald Arkell, *A Perfect Lady*
(poem in *Green Fingers*)

I'm as pure as the driven slush.

Tallulah Bankhead

To the pure, all things are unpure.

Mark Twain

I used to be Snow White … but I drifted.

Mae West

Reading

The man who does not read good books
has no advantage over the man who can't
read them.

Anonymous

There is a great deal of difference
between the eager man who wants to
read a book and the tired man who wants
a book to read.

G.K. Chesterton

We read to say what we have read.

Charles Lamb

The chief knowledge that a man gets from
reading books is the knowledge that very
few of them are worth reading.

H.L. Mencken

Relatives

Distant relatives are the best kind, and the further the better.

Frank McKinney ('Kin') Hubbard

Th' richer a relative is th' less he bothers you.

Frank McKinney ('Kin') Hubbard,
Abe Martin's Primer

[Friends are] God's apology for relations.

Hugh Kingsmill

Relations never lend one any money, and won't give one credit, even for genius. They are a sort of aggravated form of the public.

Oscar Wilde

Rich and poor

How easy it is for a man to die rich, if he
will but be contented to live miserable.

Henry Fielding

It doesn't matter
whether you're
rich or whether
you're poor – as
long as you have
money.

Max Miller

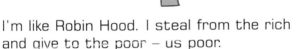

I'm like Robin Hood. I steal from the rich
and give to the poor – us poor.

Line from film ***Poppy***.
Spoken by **W.C. Fields**

The only thing that can console one for
being poor is extravagance. The only thing
that can console one for being rich is
economy.

Oscar Wilde

Rules and regulations

Regulations [are] written for the obedience of fools and the guidance of wise men.

Anonymous

The rule is, jam tomorrow and jam yesterday – but never jam today.

Lewis Carroll, *Through the Looking-Glass and What Alice Found There*

Learn all the rules, every one of them, so that you will know how to break them.

Irvin S. Cobb

The golden rule is that there are no golden rules.

George Bernard Shaw, *Man and Superman*

The Scots

The bagpipes sound exactly the same
when you have finished learning them as
when you start.

Thomas Beecham

The history of Scotland is one of theology
tempered by homicide.

Ivor Brown

On Freud's theory that a good joke will lead to
great relief and elation:

The trouble with Freud is that he never
played the Glasgow Empire Saturday
night.

Ken Dodd

Boswell:
I do indeed come from Scotland, but
I cannot help it ...

Johnson:
That, Sir, I find, is what a very great many
of your countrymen cannot help.

Samuel Johnson

That garret of the earth – that knuckle-
end of England – that land of Calvin,
oatcakes and sulphur.

Sydney Smith

Self-importance

The world has treated me very well – but
then I haven't treated it so badly either.

Noël Coward

Talk to a man about himself and he will
listen for hours.

Benjamin Disraeli

He that falls in love with himself, will have
no rivals.

Benjamin Franklin, *Poor Richard's Almanack*

Don't talk about yourself, it will be done
when you leave.

Addison Mizner

To love oneself is the beginning of a
lifelong romance.

Oscar Wilde, *An Ideal Husband*

Sex

Sex between a man and a woman can be wonderful – provided you get between the right man and the right woman.

Woody Allen

The psychiatrist asked me if I thought sex was dirty and I said, 'It is if you're doing it right.'

Woody Allen, (Line from his film *Take the Money and Run*)

Do you think that sex ought to take place before the wedding? No, not if it delays the ceremony ...

Anonymous

To an admirer:

I'll come and make love to you at five
o'clock. If I'm late start without me.

Tallulah Bankhead

A little still she strove, and much
    repented,
And whispering 'I will ne'er consent' –
    consented.

Lord Byron, *Don Juan* (poem)

He had ambitions, at one time, to become
a sex maniac, but he failed his practical.

Les Dawson

I like to wake up feeling a new man.

Jean Harlow

I am always looking for meaningful one-
night stands.

Dudley Moore

Sexual orientation

Written by another hand under the graffito, 'My mother made me a homosexual':

If I got her the wool, would she make me one?

Anonymous

I became one of the stately homos of England.

Quentin Crisp, *The Naked Civil Servant*

He was into animal husbandry – until they caught him at it.

Tom Lehrer

I'm all for bringing back the birch, but only between consenting adults in private.

Gore Vidal

Show business

Every crowd has a silver lining.

P.T. Barnum

Show business is dog eat dog. It's worse than dog eat dog. It's dog doesn't return other dog's phone calls.

Line from film *Crimes and Misdemeanors*.
Spoken by **Alan Alda**

All you need to be a success in show business is about seventeen good breaks.

Walter Matthau

Sin

When asked what a clergyman had said in his sermon on sin:

He was against it.

Calvin Coolidge

To err is human – but it feels divine.

Mae West

The only difference between a saint and a sinner is that every saint has a past, and every sinner has a future.

Oscar Wilde, *A Woman of No Importance*

Smoking

A straw with a light on one end and a
fool on the other, that's what he called
a cigarette.

Anonymous

A good cigar is as great a comfort to a
man as a good cry to a woman.

Edward Bulwer-Lytton

It has always been my rule never to
smoke when asleep and never to refrain
when awake.

Mark Twain

To cease smoking is the easiest thing
I ever did; I ought to know because I've
done it a thousand times.

Mark Twain

Speech-making

Accustomed as I am to public speaking,
I know the futility of it.

Franklin P. Adams

My dear friends – I will not call you ladies
and gentlemen, since I know you too well.

Anonymous

Speeches are like babies – easy to
conceive but hard to deliver.

Aristotle

The head cannot take in more than the
seat can endure.

Winston S. Churchill

I'm going to make a long speech because
I've not had time to prepare a short one.

Winston S. Churchill

Desperately accustomed as I am to public speaking ...

Noël Coward

If you haven't struck oil in your first three minutes, *stop boring!*

George Jessel, *Dais Without End*

It usually takes me more than three weeks to prepare a good impromptu speech.

Mark Twain

There is but one pleasure in life equal to that of being called on to make an after-dinner speech, and that is not being called on to make one.

Charles Dudley Warner

Stupidity

To call you stupid would be an insult to stupid people. I've known sheep that could outwit you. I've worn dresses with higher IQs. But you think you're an intellectual, don't you, ape?

Line from film *A Fish Called Wanda*.
Spoken by **Jamie Lee Curtis**

Genius may have its limitations, but stupidity is not thus handicapped.

Elbert Hubbard

Success

On the door to success it says: push and pull.

Anonymous

The higher the monkey climbs, the more he shows his tail.

Anonymous

If at first you don't succeed – failure may be your thing.

George Burns

If at first you don't succeed – you're fired.

Lew Grade

It is not enough to succeed. Others must fail.

Gore Vidal

163

Talkativeness

You know, you haven't stopped talking since I came here. You must have been vaccinated with a phonograph needle.

Line from film *Duck Soup*.
Spoken by **Groucho Marx**

And 'tis remarkable, that they
Talk most who have the least to say.

Matthew Prior, *Alma: or the Progress of the Mind* (poem)

I like to do all the talking myself. It saves time and prevents arguments.

Oscar Wilde, *The Remarkable Rocket* (story in *The Happy Prince and Other Tales*)

The only possible form of exercise is to talk, not to walk.

Oscar Wilde

aste

There's no accounting for tastes, as the woman said when somebody told her her son was wanted by the police.

Franklin P. Adams

Everyone to his taste, as the woman said when she kissed her cow.

Anonymous

He has impeccable bad taste.

Otis Ferguson

I have the simplest tastes. I am always satisfied with the best.

Oscar Wilde

Tax

Count that day won when, turning on its axis, this earth imposes no additional taxes.

Franklin P. Adams

The hardest thing in the world is to understand income tax.

Albert Einstein

If you get up early, work late, and pay your taxes, you will get ahead – if you strike oil.

J. Paul Getty

The avoidance of taxes is the only pursuit that still carries any reward.

John Maynard Keynes

What is the difference between a taxidermist and a tax collector?
The taxidermist takes only your skin.

Mark Twain

Teenagers

Never lend your car to anyone to whom you have given birth.

Erma Bombeck

The invention of the teenager was a mistake. Once you identify a period of life in which people get to stay out late but don't have to pay taxes – naturally, no one wants to live any other way.

Judith Martin

The best way to keep children home is to make the home atmosphere pleasant – and let the air out of the tires.

Dorothy Parker

Television

TV ... is our latest medium – we call it a medium because nothing's well done.

Goodman Ace

Television – a device that permits people who haven't anything to do to watch people who can't do anything.

Fred Allen

The bland leading the bland.

Anonymous

Television is an invention that permits you to be entertained in your living room by people you wouldn't have in your home.

David Frost

Temptation

The only way to get rid of a temptation is
to yield to it.

Oscar Wilde, *The Picture of Dorian Gray*

I can resist everything except temptation.

Oscar Wilde, *Lady Windermere's Fan*

Fastidiousness is the ability to resist a
temptation in the hope that a better one
will come along.

Oscar Wilde

Toasts

Here's to the best years of our lives,
Passed in the arms of other men's wives
— our mothers!

Anonymous

To our sweethearts and wives. May they
never meet.

Anonymous

'Gentlemen, lift the seat' ... perhaps it's
a loyal toast?

Jonathan Miller, *The Heat-Death of the
Universe* (skit in *Beyond the Fringe*)

Travel

Well, you go Uruguay, and I'll go mine.

Line from film *Animal Crackers*.
Spoken by **Groucho Marx**

Definition: I am traveller, you are a tourist, *they* are trippers.

Anonymous

In America there are two classes of travel – first class, and with children.

Robert Benchley, *Pluck and Luck*

I have found out that there ain't no surer way to find out whether you like people or hate them than to travel with them.

Mark Twain, *Tom Sawyer Abroad*

Trust

Trust him no further than you can throw him.

Anonymous

In God we trust, all others [must] pay cash.

Anonymous

Never trust a man who speaks well of everybody.

John Churton Collins

After being acquitted of drug-dealing:

I have aged 600 years and my life as a hard-working industrialist is in tatters. Would you buy a used car from me?

John De Lorean

Truth

It is always the best policy to speak the
truth, unless of course you are an
exceptionally good liar.

Jerome K. Jerome

Truth is always
duller than fiction.

Piers Paul Read

My way of joking is to tell
the truth; it's the funniest
joke in the world.

George Bernard Shaw,
John Bull's Other Island

If one tells the truth, one is
sure, sooner or later, to be found out.

Oscar Wilde

Virginity

My dad told me, 'Anything worth having is worth waiting for.' I waited until I was fifteen.

Zsa Zsa Gabor

Romance on the High Seas was Doris Day's first picture; that was before she became a virgin.

Oscar Levant, *Memoirs of an Amnesiac*

Nature abhors a virgin – a frozen asset.

Clare Boothe Luce

Wales and the Welsh

Welshmen prize their women so highly
that they put a picture of their mother-in-
law on the national flag.

Anonymous

A Welshman is a man who prays on his
knees on Sundays and preys on his
neighbours all the rest of the week.

Anonymous

The Welsh are the Italians in the rain.

Anonymous

The land of my fathers – my fathers can
have it.

Dylan Thomas

There are still parts of Wales where the only concession to gaiety is a striped shroud.

Gwyn Thomas

We can trace nearly all the disasters of English history to the influence of Wales.

Evelyn Waugh, *Decline and Fall*

War

La guerre, c'est une chose trop grave
pour la confier à des militaries

[War is too serious a business to be left
to the generals].

Georges Clemenceau

Sometime they'll give a war and nobody
will come.

Carl Sandburg

I launched the phrase 'the war to end
war' and that was not the least of my
crimes.

H.G. Wells

As long as war is regarded as wicked, it
will always have its fascination. When it
is looked upon as vulgar, it will cease to
be popular.

Oscar Wilde, *The Critic as Artist* (essay)

Wealth

If you would know what the Lord God thinks of money, you have only to look at those to whom He gave it.

Maurice Baring

Money is honey, my little sonny,
A rich man's joke is always funny.

T.E. Brown, *The Doctor* (poem)

Mother told me a couple of years ago, 'Sweetheart, settle down and marry a rich man.' I said, 'Mom, I am a rich man.'

Cher

He does not possess wealth; it possesses him.

Benjamin Franklin, *Poor Richard's Almanack*

Weather

The weather will be cold. There are
two reasons for this. One is that the
temperatures will be lower.

Anonymous (radio weather forecaster)

When two Englishmen meet, their first
talk is of the weather.

Samuel Johnson

'Tis very warm weather when one's
in bed.

Jonathan Swift, *Journal to Stella*

Everybody talks about the weather but
nobody does anything about it.

Charles Dudley Warner

Wives

They say a woman should be a cook in the kitchen and a whore in bed. Unfortunately, my wife is a whore in the kitchen and a cook in bed.

Anonymous

To Lady Astor, who had said, 'If you were my husband, I'd poison your coffee':

If you were my wife, I'd drink it.

Winston S. Churchill

I've never yet met a man who could look after me. I don't need a husband. What I need is a wife.

Joan Collins

A good wife is good, but the best wife is not so good as no wife at all.

Thomas Hardy

I have learned that only two things are necessary to keep one's wife happy. First, let her think she's having her way. And second, let her have it.

Lyndon B. Johnson

Take my wife – please!

Henny Youngman

Women

Women should be obscene and not heard.

Anonymous

A woman without a man is like a fish without a bicycle.

Anonymous

Brigands demand your money or your life; whereas women require both.

Samuel Butler

Do you know why God withheld the sense of humour from women? That we may love you instead of laughing at you.

Mrs Patrick Campbell

Can you imagine a world without men?
No crime and lots of happy, fat women.

Nicole Hollander

Woman was God's second mistake.

Friedrich Wilhelm Nietzsche, *Der Antichrist*

A woman is like a teabag. It's only when
she's in hot water that you realize how
strong she is.

Nancy Reagan

A woman's place is in the wrong.

James Thurber

In a world without men, there would be
no war – just intense negotations every
28 days.

Robin Williams

Work

Anyone can do any amount of work provided it isn't the work he is supposed to be doing at that moment.

Robert Benchley

The dictionary is the only place where success comes before work.

Arthur Brisbane

I like work: it fascinates me. I can sit and look at it for hours. I love to keep it by me: the idea of getting rid of it nearly breaks my heart.

Jerome K. Jerome, *Three Men in a Boat*

And so we plough along, as the fly said to the ox.

Henry Wadsworth Longfellow

It's true, hard work never killed anybody,
but I figure, why take the chance?

Ronald Reagan

Work is the curse of the drinking classes.

Oscar Wilde

Hard work is simply the refuge of people
who have nothing better to do.

Oscar Wilde, *The Remarkable Rocket*
(story in *The Happy Prince and Other Tales*)

Youth

There's nothing wrong with the younger generation that becoming taxpayers won't cure.

Dan Bennett

Only the young die good.

Oliver Herford

The secret of staying young is mixing with older people.

Ronnie Scott

Youth is too important to be wasted on the young.

George Bernard Shaw

No wise man ever wished to be younger.

Jonathan Swift, *Thoughts on Various Subjects*

To get back my youth I would do anything in the world, except take exercise, get up early, or be respectable.

Oscar Wilde, *The Picture of Dorian Gray*

The youth of America is their oldest tradition. It has been going on now for three hundred years.

Oscar Wilde, *A Woman of No Importance*

First published in the UK in 2003 exclusively for
WHSmith
Greenbridge Road
Swindon SN3 3LD
www.WHSmith.co.uk

by The Orion Publishing Group
5 Upper St Martin's Lane
London
WC2H 9EA

A CIP record for this book is available from the British Library

Design and typesetting by SMPS Ltd, Haverhill, Suffolk
Illustrations by Sue Blundell

ISBN 1898799598

Printed in Italy